THE LITTLE BOOK OF SLOW COOKER TIPS

ANDREW LANGLEY

First published in Great Britain in 2013 by
Absolute Press, an imprint of Bloomsbury Publishing Plc
Scarborough House, 29 James Street West
Bath BA1 2BT, England
Phone +44 (0)1225 316013 **Fax** +44 (0)1225 445836
E-mail info@absolutepress.co.uk
Web www.absolutepress.co.uk

A catalogue record of this book is available from the British Library
ISBN 13: 9781472903617
Printed and bound by Tallers Gràfics Soler, Spain

Bloomsbury Publishing Plc
50 Bedford Square, London WC1B 3DP | www.bloomsbury.com

1

‘O, scent of the daubes of my childhood!’

Pierre Huguenin

French food writer and journalist, 1936

Slow-cooked food is calming and reassuring

– for the cook. There is little in the way of split-second timing, complex manoeuvring or dramatic effects. You just put the food in the pot and

leave it to simmer away

very gently. Most of the work can be done at your convenience – and you can be confident that the result will be terrific.

2

A slow cooker does a lot more than stews.

The classic hot-pot is just one of a staggering variety of dishes. You can bake cakes and bread, prepare soups and fondues, steam Christmas puddings, make lemon curd and pâté, and produce very good meringues. Take advantage of this amazing versatility.

3

Buy a slow cooker with a thermostat.

This will switch on and off to maintain a steady maximum temperature in the pot. Research has shown that – contrary to most people's assumptions – slow cookers which are heating all the time actually save very little energy, compared with an oven. And that, of course, is half the point of buying one.

4

Make the most of cheaper ingredients.

Slow cooking gets the very best out of items which are generally seen as inferior. This is especially true of meat. A long slow cook transforms cheap cuts such as oxtail, shin of beef or neck of lamb from something unpromising and gristley into a melting marvel of succulence.

5

As a general rule, **stick closely to the liquid levels specified in the recipe.** Slow cookers allow foods to retain a lot more moisture than pans on hobs or in ovens, as the low temperature means that there is less evaporation. If you add extra liquid, it could make the eventual dish too runny,

6

It is important to

keep the cooker at a steady temperature.

If you are putting in frozen meat, for example, this will cause a sudden loss of heat in the pot and disrupt the cooking of the ingredients already there. To soften this effect, add a cupful of warm water and stir it in with the frozen meat. Better still, thaw the items thoroughly first.

7

Look after your slow cooker pot.

Most pots – earthenware or metal – are suitable for washing in a dishwasher. Or you can clean them with hot water and detergent (avoid abrasive cleaners and scouring pads altogether). Remember to rinse out well with fresh water to remove any soapy taste.

8

Surprisingly, **meats tend to cook faster than vegetables** in a slow cooker, because they need a lower temperature to get going. So most vegetables should be sliced or chopped fairly small, otherwise they may remain fairly hard. Place them at the bottom and sides of the pot, where there will be a little more heat.

9

If using very fatty meat, sauté it first at a gentle heat

in a frying pan. Turn off the heat and leave for 5 minutes. The melted fat can then be drained off (though strain carefully, so as to save the actual meat juices). This works especially well with minced lamb, which you can't trim of fat any other way.

10

Slow cookers are perfect for making stocks,

whether vegetable or meat. The essence of stock-making is a slow build of heat to get the liquid to a point where it's just barely simmering. This allows the ingredients to leach their essences into the water without losing aroma and flavour. It also makes it easier to isolate and skim off fats and scum.

11

To make a meat stock,

switch the cooker to high. Put in beef, chicken or veal bones. Chop an onion, a stick of celery, a carrot, 3 garlic cloves and a tomato and add those. Bung in 3 bay leaves, 6 peppercorns, dried thyme and parsley stalks. Just cover with water, put on the lid and switch the cooker to low.

Cook for at least 10 hours.

12

Always fill the slow cooker pot at least half way up.

Most cookers are heated by elements embedded in the casing around the sides, rather than from the base. So, if you only put in enough to cover the bottom, the heat will take a long time to reach it. The overall cooking times will have to be extended to compensate for this.

13

How big a cooker should you buy?

For one or two people, a 1.5 litre (3 pints) capacity may be enough. For two to four people, a capacity of 2.5 litres (5 pints) will be better suited. It is large enough to hold a moderate chicken. But for the more ambitious, 6.5 litres (13 pints) gives huge versatility and size. Eat half of a dish and freeze the rest.

14

A slow cooker needs a steady environment

– preferably warm and sheltered. Draughts from windows or doors, or cold conditions, can make it operate less efficiently. Place it on a hard, stable surface which is heat-resistant, as the base gets hot. Be prepared for the odd spit and spot of cooking juice to dribble out when using the high setting.

15

Here's **the quickest way of using a slow cooker.**

Simply switch it on to the high setting. Assemble and prepare the ingredients. Put in the vegetables first, then the meat or fish, then herbs and seasonings. Add stock or water to cover (just), cover and switch to low. Cook for the minimum time (specified in the manual or recipe) – about 3 hours.

16

Prepare the ingredients immediately before cooking.

Some guides tell you to get everything ready the night before. This may sound more convenient, but prepared food tends to spoil rapidly. Peeled and chopped vegetables lose vitamins, flavour and nutritional value much more quickly than whole ones.

17

If you must prep the ingredients and leave them overnight, cover them and **store in the fridge.**

This will keep them reasonably fresh. If you leave them in the slow cooker pot at room temperature, they will start to deteriorate at once. This is especially true of raw meat or fish, which can develop harmful bacteria very quickly if left in a warm place.

18

The Browning Version:

sauté the ingredients first to get a **tastier casserole.** This takes longer, but it's worth it. Follow the sequence in Tip #14, but brown the ingredients gently in a frying pan with a little oil before you add to the pot. Vegetables go first, then the meat – each for 5–10 minutes. Herbs and other flavourings go straight in the pot at the end.

19

Leave the lid in place once the cooking has begun.

The cooker – being by definition slow – takes some time to crank up to the correct temperature. As it does, steam rises and condenses on the lid, forming a delicate seal round the rim. If you lift the lid, you will break this and allow heat to escape. Allow an extra 10 minutes' cooking time.

20

Some ingredients, like meat and pulses, **are ideal for the long cooking** treatment. Others, such as pasta, shellfish and dairy products, are easily over-cooked and demand a much shorter period. So add them towards the very end of the process, when they can be cooked for 30 minutes or much less, depending on the recipe.

21

One secret of

a superb ratatouille is a long cooking time.

Another is: brown the ingredients separately first. So, sweat sliced onion and garlic in a pan with olive oil. Put in the pot. Do the same with aubergine (salted first), courgette (ditto), red and green peppers. Add a tin of tomatoes, oregano and bay leaves, and cook on low for about 7 hours.

22

Really fresh ingredients make the best vegetable stock. Chop onions, carrots, celery, tomatoes, garlic and mushrooms and put them in the pot. Add 2 bay leaves, some thyme and parsley, and 10 peppercorns. Cover with cold water and cook on the low setting for at least 10 hours. Then strain the contents through a big sieve or colander.

23

A classic *daube*, or casserole, needs shin of beef. Brown onions and put in the pot. Add chopped carrot, celery and garlic. Cut the beef into biggish chunks, dust with flour and brown. Put these in the pot. Deglaze the pan with ½ bottle of red wine, then pour that in, with beef stock to cover. Add orange zest, thyme and bay leaves. Cook long.

24

Dried beans and other large pulses should be **soaked in cold water overnight.**

Next day, drain, put in a saucepan, cover with water and bring to the boil. Drain again and rinse (this gets rid of the agents which may cause wind). Now you can put them in the slow cooker. Lentils are fine without any soaking or pre-boiling.

25

Too much liquid? Novice slow cookers are often surprised by the volume of juices produced by apparently dry ingredients like meat and vegetables, adding to whatever liquid they put in at the start. You can **reduce this by taking off the lid** half an hour before the specified time, and turning the setting to high.

26

Good thick salmon steaks slow-cook perfectly. Wipe olive oil inside the pot and put in 4 salmon steaks. In a pan, heat the juice of a lemon, a cup of water, salt, pepper, bay leaf, parsley, chopped garlic and dill. Simmer for 5 minutes, then pour over the salmon, with a dash of sesame oil and butter. Cook on the low setting for 3 hours.

27

Fish stock must be boiled for a short time, or it will become bitter and cloudy. Put chopped onion, leek, carrot and celery in the pot. Add 900g (2lb) fish heads, skin, bones and any other trimmings (from white fish only, not oily ones), plus bay leaves. Cover with water. Cook on high for 1 hour, then low for 1 hour. Strain and cool quickly.

28

Amazingly (and with care), **you can slow cook a steak.** Salt and oil a thick T-bone or club steak: cover and leave overnight at room temperature. Next day, sear the steak on all sides in a grill pan, for about 10 minutes maximum. Then transfer to the pot. Set to low and cook (or barely cook) for 40 minutes. Serve with sautéed garlic, onions, peppers and tomatoes.

29

Squid should be cooked either very fast – or very slow.

Gently brown sliced onion and garlic in olive oil in a pan. Transfer to the pot, add a big handful of spinach (or a mixture of greens), a cupful of tomato passata, and prepared squid pieces. Cook at medium or high for one hour. Let stand for 10 minutes, then serve with more oil and bread.

30

To make a simple pâté,

first set the cooker to high. Mix sausagemeat, chopped sautéed chicken livers and chopped garlic, mushrooms and olives. Season with thyme or oregano. Spoon into a bowl and cover with foil. Lower this into the pot and pour in hot water to come halfway up the sides. Cook for 4 hours, lift out immediately to cool.

31

Cheese fondue is back – and it **demands slow cooking.** Rub a garlic clove round the pot. Pour in a cup of dry white wine and set to low. Grate 280g (10oz) each of Gruyère and Emmenthal, mix with 1 tablespoon of cornflour and stir in with the wine. Add nutmeg and pepper and cook for 2 hours. Just before serving, stir in a glass of kirsch (essential).

32

Neck of lamb is cheap and slow cooks deliciously.

Brown a chopped onion, plus 1.5 kg (3lb) of floured lamb chunks and put in the pot. Deglaze pan with a slosh of sherry and pour that in, along with garlic, bay leaves, thyme, and enough water to cover. Cook for 8 hours on low, adding 4 trimmed and quartered globe artichokes 20 minutes from the end.

33

Can you fit a **leg of lamb in your slow cooker?** If so, you can **pot-roast it.**

Chop together rosemary, garlic and anchovies, and stick the mixture in small cuts in the meat. Brown the leg thoroughly and then put in the pot, adding a little reduced lamb stock. Cook on the low setting for 10 hours.

34

Roast chicken could hardly be simpler.

Season out and in with salt, pepper and tarragon. Shove a lemon (halved) inside. Rub with olive oil and place the bird in the pot. Cook on the high setting for 3 hours, then down to low for another 5 hours. More liquid is unnecessary – the chicken will produce its own.

35

Hearty bean casserole – it's what slow cookers were made for. Cook 450g (1lb) cannellini or haricot beans (as shown in Tip #24). Put in the pot with tomato passata, a slosh of white wine and a teaspoon of soy sauce. Add chopped celery, parsnips, carrots, onion and mushrooms. Season and cover with vegetable stock. Cook for 7 hours on low.

36

Pheasant needs long cooking and steady moisture. Sweat chopped onion, celery, mushrooms and bacon in butter. Put in the pot and quickly brown a brace of pheasants. Add to the veg, with bay leaves, nutmeg and thyme. Deglaze the pan with chicken stock, white wine and a squeeze of tomato purée. Pour over the birds and cook on high for 4 hours.

37

For a fine fish stew, soften sliced onion and green pepper in olive oil. Transfer to the pot, and add about 600g (1¼ lb) of fish fillets (bass, whiting, bream, gurnard and some squid). Top with olives, garlic, oregano and pepper, and cover with fish stock or white wine (or both). Cook on the low setting for 3 hours. **Serve with aioli** and fresh bread.

38

No potato dish beats **gratin dauphinoise.**

Peel 1kg (2lb) potatoes and slice thinly. Lay out on paper towels, dry and season. Put in the pot, and pour over 250ml (½ pint) of hot milk and the same of double cream. Pop in garlic and nutmeg, and cook on the low setting for 7 hours or until soft.

39

Here's a heavenly desert from Turkey.

Peel, core and halve 4 quinces. Put everything in the pot and cook on low for 7 hours. Cool and move only the quince halves to a dish. Strain the liquid in the pot and boil down by a half. Pour this over the fruit and refrigerate. Serve with drained yogurt or crème fraîche and toasted flaked almonds.

40

There's **no skin on this rice pudding** – and it's beautifully creamy. Butter the inside of the pot, and put in 55g (2oz) each of pudding rice and caster sugar. Stir in 500ml (1 pint) of whole milk and 125ml (¼ pint) of double cream. Grate nutmeg on top and cook on the low setting for 8 hours. A stir or two near the end will freshen it up before serving.

41

The **gentle heat** of the slow cooker is **ideal for clarifying butter into ghee.** This has a host of uses, particularly in South Asian cookery. Simply put three 250g (½ lb) slabs of unsalted butter in the pot and heat on the low setting for 1 hour. Carefully skim off the scum from the top, then strain the clear butter through cheesecloth. Keep in the fridge.

42

Steam your Christmas pudding

in the slow cooker, and free up oven space for the turkey. In October, pack your usual pudding mixture in a pudding basin (not quite full). Cover with foil and string. Lower into the pot and pour in boiling water to near the top. Cook on high for 12 hours. On the big day, reheat by steaming for another 4 hours on high.

43

A slow cooker **heats mulled wine without boiling it** – this way you preserve more of the alcohol. Pour 2 bottles of red wine into the pot. Add the zest and juice of 2 lemons, plus 2 cinnamon quills and an orange studded with cloves. Heat on the high setting for 1 hour. Stir in 100g (3oz) white sugar and a slug of brandy, and serve.

44

Make a tangy lemon curd.

In a pan, slowly melt 100g (3oz) unsalted butter, then stir in 220g (8oz) caster sugar and the juice of 4 unwaxed lemons. Finally, add 4 well-beaten eggs and combine thoroughly. Put the mixture in a basin and cover with foil. Lower into the pot and fill with boiling water halfway up. Cook on low for 3½ hours. Stir, allow to cool and put in jars.

45

Homemade tomato ketchup is healthier.

Skin, seed and chop 2kg (4lb) tomatoes and 2 onions. Cook in the pot on high for 1 hour. Whizz the mixture in a blender and return to the pot, adding 150ml (¼ pint) cider vinegar, 55g (2oz) sugar, a cinnamon quill, bay leaves, peppercorns, and ground allspice and cloves. Cook on low for another 8 hours.

46

Slow cooker – yogurt maker!

Pour 2 litres (4 pints) of whole cream milk into the pot and heat on the low setting for 2 hours. Check the temperature with a cooking thermometer – it should be no hotter than 43°C. Turn the setting to warm. Stir in 125g (8oz) of unflavoured live yogurt and leave for up to 6 hours. Cool and refrigerate.

47

Use your slow cooker as an air freshener.

Half-fill the pot with water, and add 2 tablespoons of baking soda plus some drops of an essential oil such as lavender. Leave the lid off and switch the cooker to high for 30 minutes. The resulting steam will rid the room, even the house, of lingering cooking smells – or worse.

48

Here are **two things to avoid once the food is cooked.** The first is touching the base unit soon after removing the pot: it will be very hot! The second is using the slow cooker to re-heat previously cooked food. This is also hazardous, as pre-cooked food needs a good quick blast of heat on the hob to zap any harmful bacteria. Slow cookers are not zappers.

49

For the ultimate slow experience, try *sous-vide*.

(French for 'in a vacuum'). You simply package the ingredients in an airtight bag, pop this into a water bath cooker, and cook very slowly for a long time (up to three days, in some cases!). Sous-vide cookers are very pricey, but are reliable and retain all the flavours, with a strong whiff of Blumenthal.

50

Cook pots take the swelter out of summer.

Cooking a meal on a stove during a heat wave can be pretty frazzling. Use a slow cooker instead, which is built to keep its minimal amount of heat inside, rather than radiating it round the kitchen. You'll find it a lot cooler.

Andrew Langley

Andrew Langley is a knowledgeable food and drink writer. Among his formative influences he lists a season picking grapes in Bordeaux, several years of raising sheep and chickens in Wiltshire and two decades drinking his grandmother's tea. He has written books on a number of Scottish and Irish whisky distilleries and is the editor of the highly regarded anthology of the writings of the legendary Victorian chef Alexis Soyer.

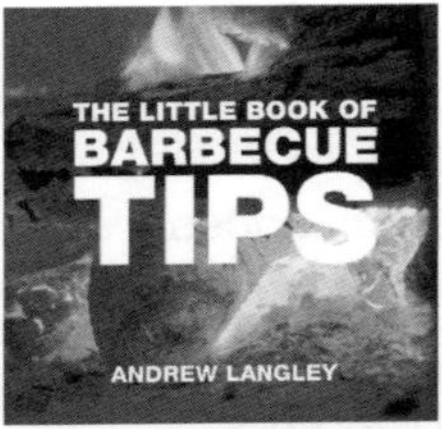
THE LITTLE BOOK OF
BARBECUE
TIPS
ANDREW LANGLEY

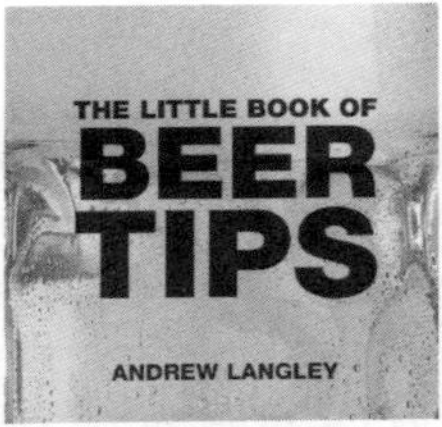
THE LITTLE BOOK OF
BEER
TIPS
ANDREW LANGLEY

THE LITTLE BOOK OF
HERB
TIPS
WILLIAM FORTT

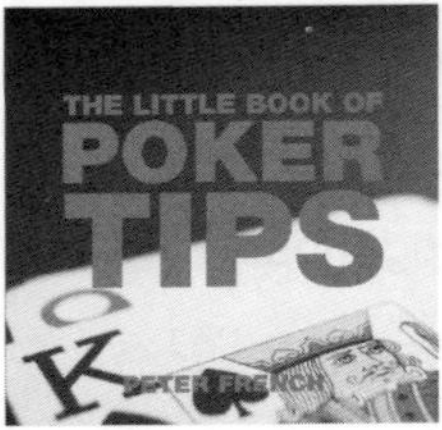
THE LITTLE BOOK OF
POKER
TIPS
PETER FRENCH

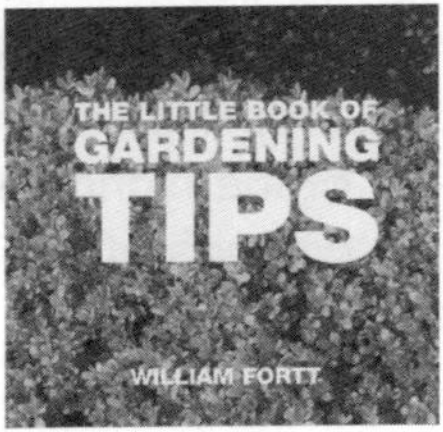
THE LITTLE BOOK OF
GARDENING
TIPS
WILLIAM FORTT

THE LITTLE BOOK OF
CHEFS'
TIPS
RICHARD MAGGS

THE LITTLE BOOK OF
SPICE
TIPS
ANDREW LANGLEY

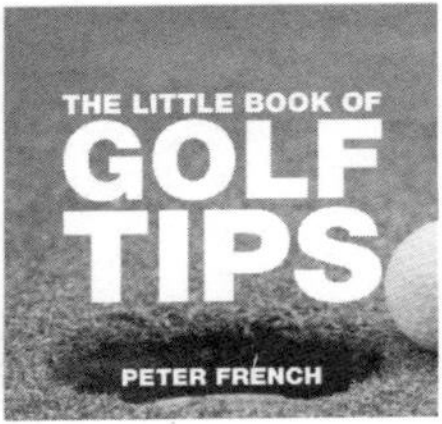
THE LITTLE BOOK OF
GOLF
TIPS
PETER FRENCH

THE LITTLE BOOK OF
TIPS
SERIES

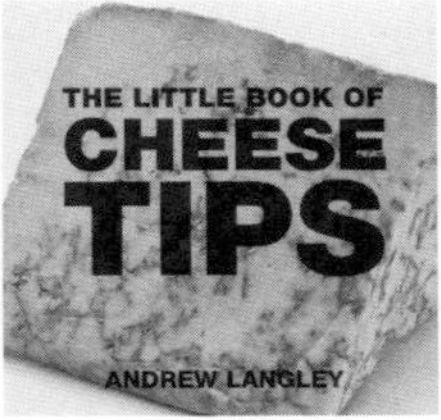
THE LITTLE BOOK OF
CHEESE
TIPS
ANDREW LANGLEY

THE LITTLE BOOK OF
WINE
TIPS
ANDREW LANGLEY

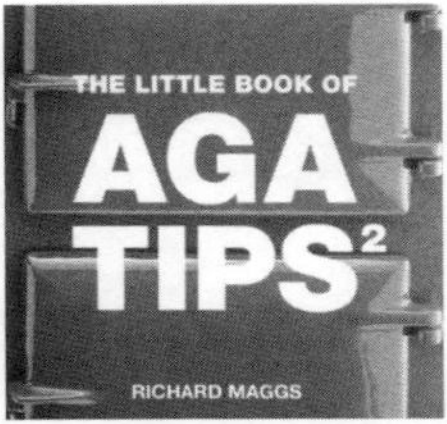
THE LITTLE BOOK OF
AGA
TIPS 2
RICHARD MAGGS

THE LITTLE BOOK OF
COFFEE
TIPS
ANDREW LANGLEY

THE LITTLE BOOK OF
TEA
TIPS
ANDREW LANGLEY

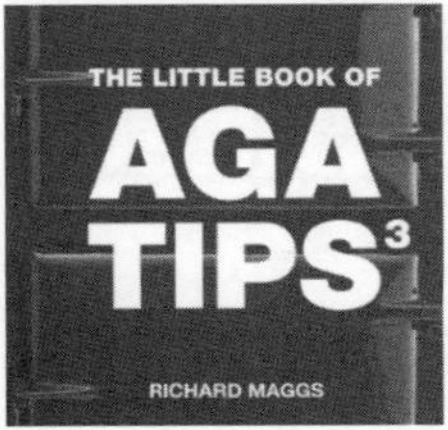
THE LITTLE BOOK OF
AGA
TIPS 3
RICHARD MAGGS

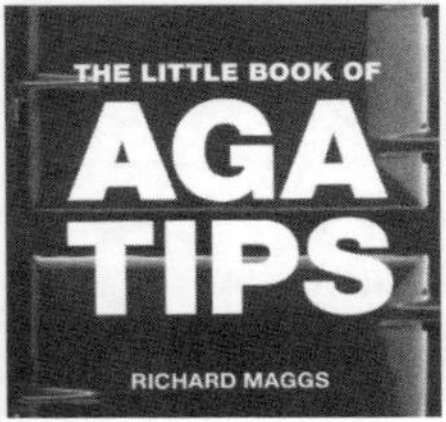
THE LITTLE BOOK OF
AGA
TIPS
RICHARD MAGGS

THE LITTLE BOOK OF
CHRISTMAS
AGA
TIPS
RICHARD MAGGS

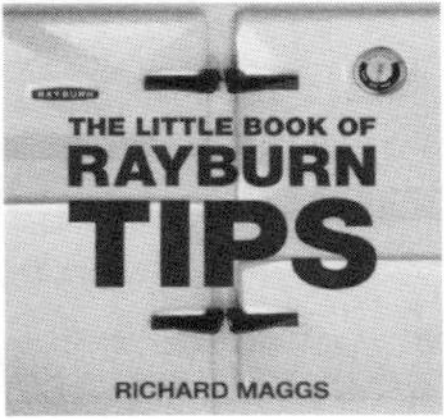
THE LITTLE BOOK OF
RAYBURN
TIPS
RICHARD MAGGS

THE LITTLE BOOK OF
BRIDGE
TIPS
PETER FRENCH

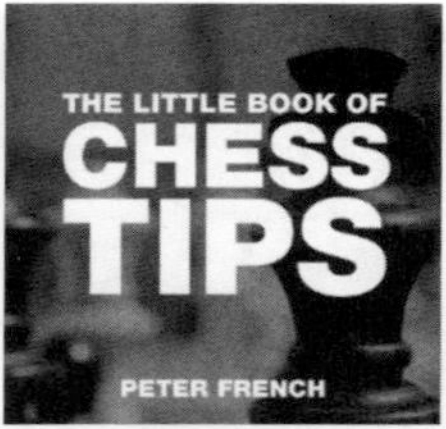
THE LITTLE BOOK OF
CHESS
TIPS
PETER FRENCH

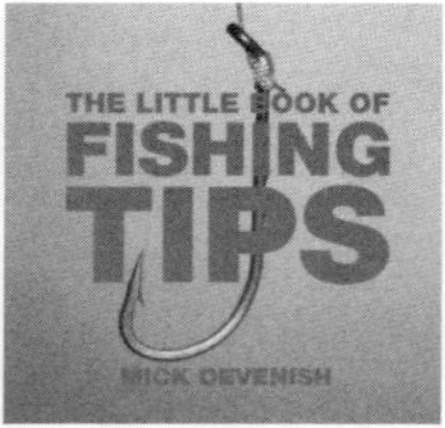
THE LITTLE BOOK OF
FISHING
TIPS
MICK DEVENISH

THE LITTLE BOOK OF
GREEN
TIPS
WILLIAM FORTT

THE LITTLE BOOK OF
KITTEN
TIPS
ANDREW LANGLEY

MARMITE
PAUL HARTLEY
THE LITTLE BOOK OF
MARMITE
TIPS

THE LITTLE BOOK OF
PUPPY
TIPS
ANDREW LANGLEY

THE LITTLE BOOK OF
WHISKY
TIPS
ANDREW LANGLEY

THE LITTLE BOOK OF
TRAVEL
TIPS
MEGAN DEVENISH

Little Books of Tips from Absolute Press

Aga Tips
Aga Tips 2
Aga Tips 3
Allotment Tips
Backgammon Tips
Barbecue Tips
Beer Tips
Bread Tips
Bread Machine Tips
Bridge Tips
Cake Baking Tips
Cake Decorating Tips
Champagne Tips
Cheese Tips
Chefs' Tips
Chess Tips
Chocolate Tips
Christmas Aga Tips
Chutney and Pickle Tips
Cocktail Tips
Coffee Tips
Cupcake Tips
Curry Tips
Fishing Tips
Fly Fishing Tips
Frugal Tips
Gardening Tips
Golf Tips
Green Tips
Grow Your Own Tips
Herb Tips
Houseplant Tips
Ice Cream Tips
Jam Tips
Kitten Tips
Macaroon Tips
Marmite Tips
Olive Oil Tips
Pasta Tips
Poker Tips
Puppy Tips
Rayburn Tips
Slow Cooker Tips
Spice Tips
Tea Tips
Travel Tips
Whisky Tips
Wine Tips
Wok Tips
Vinegar Tips